# THIS NOTEBOOK
# BELONGS TO:

______________________________

www.ingramcontent.com/pod-product-compliance
Lightning Source LLC
Chambersburg PA
CBHW030357280726
48655CB00019B/2312